The Awakening

Alyssa Michelle

Presentation by *BookLeaf Publishing*

Web: www.bookleafpub.com

E-mail: info@bookleafpub.com

ISBN: 9789358360066

First edition 2021

To my children Miliana and Ava, no dream is ever too big to accomplish.

To my soul tribe and those who are searching for light, I am thankful that we have crossed paths.

And to the woman I once was, the woman I am now and the woman I will soon be, thank you for never giving up.

Acknowledgements

It's amazing how life can align you with the right people and opportunities when you need it the most, and more importantly, when you're ready to receive it.

Thank you, Lizeth, for believing in me every step of the way and pushing me to be who I truly am.

Words cannot fully express my gratitude toward such a beautiful soul who helped cultivate something that already existed in me, which could not be seen by others.

1. The Miseducation of the Introvert

They once thought

That the absence of my voice

Meant that I didn't have one;

When in reality,

Silence became the coping mechanism

For every traumatic experience

That my subconscious recorded.

"Speak up!"

But I was always too afraid

To step on toes, ruffle feathers

And make waves

In ways that showed I had a backbone.

Losing my identity

To please others

At the cost of my own happiness

Was enough to show me

That everyone that I was batting for

Wasn't truly on my team.

"Speak up!"

They want you to do good,

Just not better than them.

To think–

That we must shrink ourselves

For the comfort of others is disheartening.

"Speak up!"

I remember when they thought

That the absence of my voice

Meant that I didn't have one;

Until the power of my truth

Broke every misconception.

2. The Healer

Every once in a while,

Someone always gives you back the light

That you once shared with the world;

And it begins to make perfect sense

That your pain was used as a catalyst

To heal.

But it had to start with you-

You are a walking testimony

And your soul bears infinite knowledge

That will carry through every
reincarnation.

But you must always remember who you
are.

3. Parenthood

The bathroom seems to be

The only place where I just might get some

peace.

As I creep away silently,

I'm hoping they didn't see me leave.

Social media scrolling on the toilet,

Hearing toddler feet scurrying,

The laughter of two daughters

And what sounds like a home filled with

love;

And at that moment,

I forgot why I even needed a moment

To get away

From the one thing

That gives me a reason to live everyday.

4. Beauty

They say that beauty is in the eye of the beholder

Which means that beauty cannot exist

Until someone comes along

And discovers it.

How absurd it is to believe

That you cannot be beautiful

Without being validated externally.

Does a flower not bloom

Because it has yet to be found?

Or a bird stop singing

Because no one hears its song?

Unless, of course,

The true power of its beauty

Is knowing

That no matter how many times

It may have been overlooked,

It already possesses

Something that you cannot remove or create

Because true beauty is innate

And divinely exists

Without judgement.

5. Wanderlust

I yearn for a place

Which I can call home;

Feelings of familiar,

As if I belong.

Lead me there through the cosmos,

In an alternate dimension,

Where time doesn't exist

And our souls become intrepid.

With silver cords keeping us connected,

Life is full of illusions

And our realities are created from our
perceptions.

Judgements and thoughts

Are merely projections

And every connection we form

Mirrors our true reflection.

Find me finding myself

In a space that is infinite

With the freedom to embody

A spirit that is adventurous.

6. Perfect Enough

I used to think that I wasn't perfect enough

To be loved,

That I needed to change the core of who I was

To be completely accepted.

And ironically,

I was loving the most imperfect parts of others,

Who would never be satisfied

Even if I sacrificed my entire life

To prove that they were perfect enough for me.

You see,

I was trying to fix myself through them

As trauma bonding

Became the psychological trap we fell in.

Deeper truths revealed to me

That our imperfections are needed

To make us complete.

That in darkness is where you truly find the
light

And without it, there is no duality.

So perfect enough

I became for myself

When I stopped filling my emotional voids

With the broken pieces of someone else.

7. Memories

What is a memory

But a reminder

Of how we can time travel through
nostalgia

To a place that will never die?

Through touch and smell,

Sight and sound,

We feel everything as if

Nothing exists outside of that moment.

A thousand memories framed

Through faces,

Bringing us back to familiar places.

When lives pass,

Memories are all we have

To bring them back.

So take the pictures

And make the plans

Because you never know

How much time you'll have left in your
hands.

8. The Right To Ascension

You don't need to ask for permission to ascend.

It's only the beginning

Even though it feels like the end.

You may have to let some people go on the way up

Who you thought were your friends.

Poisoned by envy,

The taste becomes bitter

Because they thought you'd stay the same;

But instead, you got better.

It can get lonely at the top

When you're around the wrong people,

But trust the process.

You're being redirected to souls whose
energy to yours is equal.

9. Widow Mother

How does it feel being the mother of a child
who lost their father?

It feels like never doing enough

Or spoiling her too much,

Trying to compensate

For something that she'll never tangibly
have again.

The challenge to find balance between

Sympathy and discipline,

When she throws a temper tantrum,

Then cries out how much she misses him.

As hugs suffice for the moment

With reminders that she'll always be
protected

And that through her,

Pieces of him will always remain present.

With timeless memories that live on

Through videos and photos

And that the depth of his love for her

Will remain within her heart as she grows.

It's never easy,

Accepting the truth of death

Or even for a child to completely
comprehend;

And although as a parent I feel alone,

It's apparent that his presence will forever
be known.

10. Divine Timing

They say that timing is everything

And that nothing happens by chance;

Serendipities are really synchronicities

As every experience is connected

To something beyond our own
comprehension.

Imagine

If what you went through never happened,

Would you have learned anything?

Or when that prayer that you kept faith in

Finally came with a blessing.

It never seems to happen when we want it
to;

But it always comes at the most unexpected
times,

Filling our hearts with gratitude

Through a timeline that's divine.

11. Reunion

I know he's somewhere out there

Waiting for me

As I await his arrival so patiently.

I've dreamt of the day

We'd be together for an eternity;

But only after karmic debts have been paid

Will we meet.

My soul has yearned for lifetimes

To feel your presence yet again,

Even though your identity is unknown.

Sparks will fly through eyes

During our souls' reunion.

12.   Prototype

A limited edition.

One of its own kind.

Your energy is undeniable,

It's impossible to hide.

Your tribe is attracted by your vibe

But yours attracts many;

They're in dire need of what you possess,

Swarmed like bees to honey.

It's innately placed into your DNA,

Shadow work that worked its way,

Breaking cycles

From the generational pain.

Failed attempts to imitate

The ethereal charisma

And light you emanate.

Only proves

The power of standing in your truth

As you become the prototype.

13. Forgiveness

Resentment is a weight too heavy to bear

And a poison too toxic to feed off;

The emotional attachment stunts our growth

As its hatred rights no wrongs.

How can we liberate ourselves

If we're still holding onto toxicity?

Becoming prisoners of our egos,

Suppressing our own healing?

Forgiveness is not granting the right of an injustice

Nor does it mean allowing it to happen
again,

But you owe it to yourself,

Not to give others the freedom to rent
space in your head.

So reserve your power

To liberate yourself from emotional wounds

And by doing so, you liberate someone else

To forgive themselves

And make amends with you.

14.   Dear Anxiety

Dear Anxiety,

Why do you do this to me?

As you confuse

Fight or flight

With my subconscious cues

To be triggered by the remnants of my

unhealed wounds.

Heart leaping out of my chest,

Tongue tied,

Gasping for my breath;

Thoughts scattered

As I need to be alone to decompress;

Hands trembling,

Then I remember to breathe.

It's not as bad as you make it seem,

You're such a drama Queen!

At the first sign of conflict

Always overreacting.

I am safe

And you decided to show up at the wrong
time;

Please leave me in my peace

While I ground myself with my conscious
mind.

15.   Trust

Trust is so fragile;

It can take years to build

And just one moment to be broken.

Ironic it seems

That the time we spend getting to know someone

Can reveal how little we really knew them

And so much more than we expected.

But only by learning

To truly trust ourselves

In the process.

16.   Soldier of Love

When you long to be loved

But you're scared to accept it

Because pain has been no stranger

And it's scars you've been left with,

You make up your mind

To revisit the space

Around your heart

Where you built a barricade.

You stop running from who you truly are

And what you know you deserve.

You are not one to give up.

Especially when your fight is in love's

honour.

You know it always wins,

No matter what odds it's up against.

A soldier of love you are

And you will fight until the very end.

17.   Lessons

Mistakes are just lessons in disguise,

Tests to see if what we've learned

We'll apply.

Failed attempts to do right,

Repeat plots with different characters,

Confined by Déjà Vu in a time loop,

Until we choose otherwise.

Whirlpooled

As the currents of our current

circumstances

Have us anticipating second chances.

Only to find out

That surrendering to the ebb and flow

Will cause blessings to flow

But only if we choose the right path to
follow.

Take heed to every message

As each day given provides more practice

To do better and break negative habits.

18.   Intuition

When you know something

Without having tangible proof

And a gut feeling

Stirs inside of you,

Just know, that you are not delusional.

As the crown chakra receives,

It enables the third eye to see

Far beyond what the naked eye can
perceive.

Nothing can pass

Someone who is in tune

To the highest frequencies

As channelled messages flow with ease.

But the challenge

Is teaching ourselves to believe

Our own internal compasses

As we tend to ignore the voice of truth,

Instead of following the wisdom we already encompass.

19.   Dad

For 30 years we lived

Without knowing the other one existed

Proved by Ancestry kits

And directed by divine guidance.

Strangers at first

But it took some time

To catch up

On what our lives had been like.

To my surprise,

You lived only 20 minutes away;

It was as if fate had been on our side.

How everything fell into place!

I now know

Where I get my eyes from,

But we have more in common

Than 23 pairs of chromosomes.

I'm proud of every moment spent

Creating memories that will last

And for once, I can finally say

I have someone who I can call my Dad.

20. Confidence

Transmute every failure into power

By claiming your purpose.

Your spirit is too big

To fit into places

That no longer serve your highest self

With a passion so infinite.

There is nothing wrong with doing what's
best for you

As watching eyes become critical;

Their feet are not the ones walking in your
shoes

Or heeding to the divine call.

Your mission had been preordained

Before your conception,

An agreement to fulfil

As your guides give you direction.

Have constructive reasons

To stand for what you believe in,

Knowing yourself completely

As you emulate the epitome of authenticity.

www.ingramcontent.com/pod-product-compliance
Lightning Source LLC
La Vergne TN
LVHW051232200726

843510LV00011B/1554